WILLIAM HATFIELD

WHERE ARE WE ON GOD'S TIMELINE REVISITED

ISBN: 978-1-990362-21-7

DEDICATION

I DEDICATE THIS BOOK TO THE THIRSTY AND HUNGRY SAINTS OF GOD THAT DESIRE AN INTIMACY WITH THE HOLY SPIRIT LIKE NO OTHER. MY PRAYER IS THAT YOU CAN FIND THIS JOURNEY AS A SOURCE OF ENCOURAGEMENT, STRENGTH, AND POWER TO OVERCOME LIFE'S STRUGGLES AND WALK IN A GREATER SENSE OF FREEDOM AND RELATIONSHIP WITH THE HOLY SPIRIT AND ALL WITHIN YOUR SPHERE OF INFLUENCE.

ACKNOWLEDGEMENTS

I would like to thank many people who put their ideas and understanding of the end times on social media. One individual doesn't have it all figured out, even though they like to think they do. I found God gives each of us a piece to prevent the high-minded folks from exalting themselves beyond measure.

Table of Contents

PROLOGUE

We look at life and wonder what's up with civilization. Has everyone gone nuts except me? Morals aren't what they should be. Nations are at each other's throats. Economies worldwide are bouncing up and down. I wonder if there is any significance to any of it. The first part of this book was my attempt to understand God's timeline through information supplied by history and the current state of affairs of the world by the worlds source of information. That's just its information. I find most prophecy teachers default to information they can understand.

The secret is to get revelation from the Holy Spirit as He knows all things and has viewed the entire timeline of mankind.

1 WHERE ARE WE ON GOD'S TIMELINE CONCERNING THE END

April 3, 2020, the earth is in lock down because of covid 19 pandemic. Information from news media is flowing fast and furious, and as usual bad news gets more ratings, so we hear of the many thousands that have died over and over. Only a small snip it at the end of the news show of the hundreds of thousands that have recovered. Fear seems to be doing more damage than the virus as people start hoarding and causing unnecessary shortages, especially in toilet paper. This is a virus of the breathing system not digestive and anal system. I guess fear causes people to become irrational in their thinking.

Luke 21:25 King James Version (KJV)

25 And there shall be signs in the sun, and in the moon, and in the stars; and upon the earth

distress of nations, with perplexity; the sea and the waves roaring;

Politicians are using the pandemic as a tool to blame their opponents and cause distrust and more fear. Conspiracy theories are abounding. The latest is that it came from the same area in China where they have their level 4 biological laboratories located that have released previous viruses and it was released accidently on purpose. That wouldn't surprise me in this day of selfishness and self-centeredness. Matthew 24:
12And because iniquity shall abound, the love of many shall wax cold. The conspiracy goes china was forced to sign a document saying they would no longer manipulate the stock market to get personal gain. Interesting enough all the countries that are feeling the health effects of the pandemic are suffering financially as well whereas China is actually pulling ahead of everyone fulfilling their desire to become the leader in the world financial markets. Interesting enough is China is close to being the most powerful military in the world bragging they

could put together two hundred million soldiers in about a month's time.

Interesting that bible prophecy experts have all come alive with their opinions and books to sell. It seems not only politicians take advantage of a crisis, but marketers of literature and religions do the same. You tube is full of opinions, theories, speculations and some straight-out silly ideas about this being the end of everything so go hide in a cave and store water and food so you will survive until Jesus Christ comes back to destroy the bad guys and we live happily ever after.

Jesus disciples asked him about the end of the world. In Matthew 24 the disciples used the word world which is a miss translation and should be age referring to this present age where man rules the earth.

Temple Destruction Foretold

(Mark 13:1-9; Luke 21:5-9)

Matthew 24:**1** And Jesus went out and departed

from the temple: and his disciples came to *him* for to shew him the buildings of the temple.

2 And Jesus said unto them, See ye not all these things? verily I say unto you, There shall not be left here one stone upon another that shall not be thrown down.

3 And as he sat upon the mount of Olives, the disciples came unto him privately, saying, Tell us, when shall these things be? and what *shall be* the sign of thy coming, and of the end of the world?

4 And Jesus answered and said unto them, Take heed that no man deceive you.

False Christs

5 For many shall come in my name, saying, I am
Christ; and shall deceive many. **6** And ye shall
hear of wars and rumours of wars: see that ye be
not troubled: for all *these things* must come to
pass, but the end is not yet. **7** For nation shall rise
against nation, and kingdom against kingdom:
and there shall be famines, and pestilences, and

earthquakes, in divers' places. **8** All these *are* the beginning of sorrows.

Witnessing to All Nations

(Mark 13:10-13; Luke 21:10-19)

9 Then shall they deliver you up to be afflicted and shall kill you: and ye shall be hated of all nations for my name's sake. **10** And then shall many be offended, and shall betray one another, and shall hate one another. **11** And many false prophets shall rise and shall deceive many. **12** And because iniquity shall abound, the love of many shall wax cold. **13** But he that shall endure unto the end, the same shall be saved. **14** And this gospel of the kingdom shall be preached in all the world for a witness unto all nations; and then shall the end come.

The Abomination of Desolation

(Mark 13:14-23; Luke 21:20-24)

15 When ye therefore shall see the abomination of desolation, spoken of by Daniel the prophet, stand in the holy place, (whoso readeth, let him

understand:) **16** Then let them which be in
Judaea flee into the mountains: **17** Let him which
is on the housetop not come down to take
anything out of his house: **18** Neither let him
which is in the field return back to take his
clothes. **19** And woe unto them that are with
child, and to them that give suck in those days!
20 But pray ye that your flight be not in the
winter, neither on the Sabbath day: **21** For then
shall be great tribulation, such as was not since
the beginning of the world to this time, no, nor
ever shall be. **22** And except those days should be
shortened, there should no flesh be saved: but
for the elect's sake those days shall be shortened.
23 Then if any man shall say unto you, Lo, here *is*
Christ, or there; believe *it* not. **24** For there shall
arise false Christs, and false prophets, and shall
shew great signs and wonders; insomuch that, if
it were possible, they shall deceive the very elect.

25 Behold, I have told you before.

The Return of the Son of Man

(Mark 13:24-27; Luke 21:25-28)

26 Wherefore if they shall say unto you, Behold,
he is in the desert; go not forth: behold, *he is* in
the secret chambers; believe *it* not. **27** For as the
lightning cometh out of the east, and shineth
even unto the west; so, shall also the coming of
the Son of man be. **28** For wheresoever the
carcase is there will the eagles be gathered
together.

29 Immediately after the tribulation of those
days shall the sun be darkened, and the moon
shall not give her light, and the stars shall fall
from heaven, and the powers of the heavens
shall be shaken: **30** And then shall appear the
sign of the Son of man in heaven: and then shall
all the tribes of the earth mourn, and they shall
see the Son of man coming in the clouds of
heaven with power and great glory. **31** And he
shall send his angels with the great sound of a
trumpet, and they shall gather together his elect
from the four winds, from one end of heaven to
the other.

The lesson of the Fig Tree

(Mark 13:28-31; Luke 21:29-33)

32 Now learn a parable of the fig tree; When his
branch is yet tender, and putteth forth leaves, ye
know that summer *is* nigh: **33** So likewise ye,
when ye shall see all these things, know that it is
near, *even* at the doors. **34** Verily I say unto you,
This generation shall not pass, till all these things
be fulfilled. **35** Heaven and earth shall pass away,
but my words shall not pass away.

Be Ready at Any Hour

(Genesis 6:1-7; Mark 13:32-37; Luke 12:35-48)

36 But of that day and hour knoweth no *man*, no,
not the angels of heaven, but my Father only. **37**
But as the days of Noe *were*, so shall also the
coming of the Son of man be. **38** For as in the
days that were before the flood they were eating
and drinking, marrying and giving in marriage,
until the day that Noe entered into the ark, **39**
And knew not until the flood came, and took
them all away; so, shall also the coming of the
Son of man be. **40** Then shall two be in the field;
the one shall be taken, and the other left. **41** Two

women shall be grinding at the mill; the one shall
be taken, and the other left.

42 Watch therefore: for ye know not what hour
your Lord doth come. **43** But know this that if the
good man of the house had known in what watch
the thief would come, he would have watched,
and would not have suffered his house to be
broken up. **44**Therefore be ye also ready: for in
such an hour as ye think not the Son of man
cometh.

45 Who then is a faithful and wise servant, whom
his lord hath made ruler over his household, to
give them meat in due season? **46** Blessed *is* that
servant, whom his lord when he cometh shall
find so doing.

47 Verily I say unto you, That he shall make him
ruler over all his goods. **48** But and if that evil
servant shall say in his heart, My lord delayeth his
coming; **49** And shall begin to smite *his* fellow
servants, and to eat and drink with the drunken;
50 The lord of that servant shall come in a day
when he looketh not for *him*, and in an hour that

he is not aware of,
51 And shall cut him asunder, and appoint *him*
his portion with the hypocrites: there shall be
weeping and gnashing of teeth.

True; we are in the middle of a crisis, but we have been in a lot of crisis but never got the media attention we have now.... hmmm I wonder why? Let's look at Matthew 24 and see if we have clues.

Temple in Jerusalem · Destroyed

070 AD

Matthew 24:**1** And Jesus went out and departed from the temple: and his disciples came to *him* for to shew him the buildings of the temple.

2 And Jesus said unto them, See ye not all these things? verily I say unto you, There shall not be left here one stone upon another that shall not be thrown down.

The Romans Destroy the Temple

At Jerusalem, 70 AD

In the year 66 AD the Jews of Judea rebelled against their Roman masters. In response, the Emperor Nero dispatched an army under the generalship of Vespasian to restore order. By the year 68, resistance in the northern part of the province had been eradicated and the Romans turned their full attention to the subjugation of Jerusalem. That same year, the Emperor Nero died by his own hand, creating a power vacuum in Rome. In the resultant chaos, Vespasian was declared Emperor and returned to the Imperial City. It fell to his son, Titus, to lead the remaining army in the assault on Jerusalem.

The Roman legions surrounded the city and began to slowly squeeze the life out of the Jewish stronghold. By the year 70, the attackers had breached Jerusalem's outer walls and began a systematic ransacking of the city. The assault culminated in the burning and destruction of the

Temple that served as the center of Judaism.

In victory, the Romans slaughtered thousands. Of those sparred from death: thousands more were enslaved and sent to toil in the mines of Egypt, others were dispersed to arenas throughout the Empire to be butchered for the amusement of the public. The Temple's sacred relics were taken to Rome where they were displayed in celebration of the victory.

The rebellion sputtered on for another three years and was finally extinguished in 73 AD with the fall of the various pockets of resistance including the stronghold at Masada.

"...the Jews let out a shout of dismay that matched the tragedy."

Our only first-hand account of the Roman assault on the Temple comes from the Jewish historian Josephus Flavius. Josephus was a former leader of the Jewish Revolt who had surrendered to the Romans and had won favor from Vespasian. In gratitude, Josephus took on Vespasian's family name - Flavius - as his own. We join his account as the Romans fight their way into the inner sanctum of the Temple:

"...the rebels shortly after attacked the Romans again, and a clash followed between the guards of the sanctuary and the troops who were putting out the fire inside the inner court; the latter routed the Jews and followed in hot pursuit right up to the Temple itself. Then one of the soldiers, without awaiting any orders and with no dread of so momentous a deed, but urged on by some supernatural force, snatched a blazing piece of wood and, climbing on another soldier's back, hurled the flaming brand through a low golden window that gave access, on the north side, to the rooms that surrounded the sanctuary. As the flames shot up, the Jews let out a shout of dismay that matched the tragedy; they flocked to the rescue, with no thought of sparing their lives or husbanding their strength; for the sacred structure that they had constantly guarded with such devotion was vanishing before their very eyes.

...No exhortation or threat could now restrain the

impetuosity of the legions; for passion was in supreme command. Crowded together around the entrances, many were trampled down by their companions; others, stumbling on the smoldering and smoked-filled ruins of the porticoes, died as miserably as the defeated. As they drew closer to the Temple, they pretended not even to hear Caesar's orders, but urged the men in front to throw in more firebrands. The rebels were powerless to help; carnage and flight spread throughout.

Most of the slain were peaceful citizens, weak and unarmed, and they were butchered where they were caught. The heap of corpses mounted higher and higher about the altar; a stream of blood flowed down the Temple's steps, and the bodies of those slain at the top slipped to the bottom.

When Caesar failed to restrain the fury of his frenzied soldiers, and the fire could not be checked, he entered the building with his generals and looked at the holy place of the sanctuary and all its furnishings, which exceeded by far the accounts current in foreign lands and fully justified their splendid repute in our own.

As the flames had not yet penetrated to the inner sanctum, but were consuming the chambers that surrounded the sanctuary, Titus assumed correctly that there was still time to save the structure; he ran out and by personal appeals he endeavored to persuade his men to put out the fire, instructing Liberalius, a centurion of his bodyguard of lancers, to club any of the men who disobeyed his orders. But their respect for Caesar and their fear of the centurion's staff who was trying to check them were overpowered by their rage, their detestation of the Jews, and an utterly uncontrolled lust for battle.

Most of them were spurred on, moreover, by the expectation of loot, convinced that the interior was full of money and dazzled by observing that everything around them was made of gold. But they were forestalled by one of those who had entered into the building, and who, when Caesar dashed out to restrain the troops, pushed a firebrand, in the darkness, into the hinges of the gate Then, when the flames suddenly shot up from the interior, Caesar and his generals withdrew, and no one was left to prevent those outside from kindling the blaze. Thus, in defiance of Caesar's wishes, the Temple was set on fire.

While the Temple was ablaze, the attackers plundered it, and countless people who were caught by them were slaughtered. There was no pity for age and no regard was accorded rank; children and old men, laymen and priests, alike were butchered; every class was pursued and crushed in the grip of war, whether they cried out for mercy or offered resistance.

Through the roar of the flames streaming far and wide, the groans of the falling victims were heard; such was the height of the hill and the magnitude of the blazing pile that the entire city seemed to be ablaze; and the noise - nothing more deafening and frightening could be imagined.

There were the war cries of the Roman legions as they swept onwards en masse, the yells of the rebels encircled by fire and sword, the panic of the people who, cut off above, fled into the arms of the enemy, and their shrieks as they met their fate. The cries on the hill blended with those of the multitudes in the city below; and now many people who were exhausted and tongue-tied as a result of hunger, when they beheld the Temple on fire, found strength once more to lament and wail. Peraea and the surrounding hills, added their echoes to the deafening din. But more horrifying than the din were the sufferings.

The Temple Mount, everywhere enveloped in flames, seemed to be boiling over from its base; yet the blood seemed more abundant than the flames and the numbers of the slain greater than those of the slayers. The soldiers climbed over heaps of bodies as they chased the fugitives."

References:

Josephus' account appears in: Cornfield, Gaalya ed., Josephus, The Jewish War (1982); Duruy, Victor, History of Rome vol. V (1883).

Even though the nation and Israel were destroyed in 70A.D and dispersed they came back as a nation in 1948 one thousand eight hundred and seventy-eight years later. No other nation in existence has ever been able to accomplish this. God's prophetic time clock started again. The queen of England once asked, "How do you know God exists?" She got a one-word answer

ISRAEL.

2 DECEPTIONS

3 And as he sat upon the Mount of Olives, the disciples came unto him privately, saying, Tell us, when shall these things be?" and what *shall be* the sign of thy coming, and of the end of the world?

4 And Jesus answered and said unto them, Take heed that no man deceive you

deceive

[dəˈsēv]

VERB

(of a person) cause (someone) to believe something that is not true, typically in order to gain some personal advantage.

As I started this section I just got a message on my smart phone that the government is sending money to its citizens to fight covid 19 virus and I should klik on the link to give my banking information for them to deposit the money into my bank account. Another one came through messenger for me to send her money to get her covid 19 medical card so she could get tested for

the virus. In this modern day of enhanced technology dishonest people are looking for quick gain at the expense of gullible people. But then some of these people are greedy and think they can get away accepting money that doesn't belong to them and fall for the scam only to soon realize their bank accounts have been drained. More people are self-serving and inconsiderate than ever before.

2 Timothy 3:1-5 [1]But mark this: There will be
terrible times in the last days. [2]People will be
lovers of themselves, **lovers of** money, boastful,
proud, abusive, disobedient to their parents,
ungrateful, unholy, [3]without love, unforgiving,
slanderous, without **self**-control, brutal, not
lovers of the good, [4]treacherous, rash, conceited,
lovers of pleasure rather than lovers of God

[5]having a form of godliness but denying its power. Have nothing to do with such people.

There is major deception in church congregations in this day and age. I was an associate pastor in a Filipino and it was very low key, nothing exciting, no moves of God or manifestations of the Holy Spirit. This was something I wasn't used to as my spiritual father taught me and many others about the gifts and manifestations of the Holy Spirit. However, getting married to a Filipino woman I decided to join the Filipino group and before I knew it I was given a preaching schedule and put on their board of leaders. I enjoyed trying to influence them concerning the Holy Spirit and His love and manifestations.

However, the head pastor started preaching the cessation doctrine which declares God doesn't baptize with the Holy Spirit after the last of the apostles died. God doesn't heal anymore, and no miracles are done and definitely no more speaking in tongues. I really wonder how they get around Hebrews 13:8 Jesus Christ is the same yesterday and today and forever. You know an apostasy of the faith is happening right under your nose when the Christians are promoting the doctrines of demons to justify their unbelief in God's word. It is easier to blame God for the lack of faith and carnality than stand up take responsibility for your actions and repent. Repentance is now a curse word in today's church circles. Being of a different belief system having been baptized in the Holy Spirit speaking in tongues and being used in many of the manifestations of the Holy Spirit, I decided to leave quietly. It was not my place to challenge him as I was only an associate pastor and not responsible to that denominational structure. I graciously stepped down and began the transition to new ministry opportunities.

Another form of deception in churches is exaltation of denominational heads. Some organizations may have started out as moves of God but after a few years you notice how men are dominating and controlling the flow of their congregations. Making sure a certain amount of money fills the coffers and no church within their organization will decide to go with another organization because after all they are the right organization and everyone else is a failure. I was in a bible college going to take some classes when the organizations

The Co-founder took the stage and demanded that we call her husband by the titles he had given himself. This was an act of honor on our part and if we didn't comply we would not get an audience with that man. It was all one way where the layman bowed in honor to the leadership, and nothing was returned to the laity. Our jobs were to feed their egos and we were supposed to feel honored to do so. I decided to leave that bible college as I had three years of Bible College and during the time in Bible College you are taught more what the organization believes rather than what the Bible actually says. I got paperwork from that organization says I have my diploma for advanced teaching and realized afterwards, I had to unlearn much of what the bible college taught me to flow with the Holy

Spirit.

What Christians don't realize is that the moving of the Holy Spirit isn't non-conditional on sinners because they are doing what is natural to them SINNING WITH ALL THEIR HEART AND ABILITY.

2 chronicles 7:[14] if my people, who are called by my name, will humble themselves and pray and seek my face and turn from their wicked ways, then I will hear from heaven, and I will forgive their sin and will heal their land. [15] Now my eyes will be open and my ears attentive to the prayers offered in this place.

For too long the Body of Christ has sought fame, accolades and money thus making them empire builders rather than true kingdom builders. True kingdom builders, in my opinion, are to follow the Holy Spirit wherever He leads and make your life about other people, allowing the Holy Spirit to manifest Himself through you to help others find their destinies in Christ. I don't believe God sent this pandemic rather Satan with the help of sinful people but can and will use it to get a lukewarm churches attention.

2 Peter 3:3 [3]Above all, you must understand that in the last days scoffers will come, scoffing, and following their own evil desires.

Psalm 1:1-3 [1]Blessed is the one who does not walk in step with the wicked or stand in the way that sinners take or sit in the company of **mockers**, [2]but whose delight is in the law of the LORD, and who meditates on his law day and night. [3]That person is like a tree planted by streams of water, which yields its fruit in season and whose leaf does not wither- whatever they do prosper.

It seems that you can't turn around without hearing people mock God and believers. Where I am currently residing, I find if I have a difference of opinion than this individual the first thing he does is mock me, mock God, belittle me trying to manipulate me to fulfill his own selfish desires, and insist the world system is right because they always tell the truth on the news shows. Then try to watch a television show while he is in the room, and he mocks the characters and actors and derides them with all kind of racist remarks. We find ourselves in all kinds of situations. Sometimes because of foolish choices other times forced because of life throwing you under the bus.

I find when we are in unorthodox situations it is better to walk in the fruit of the Spirit and trust God for deliverance. By walking in the fruit of the Spirit we may in some way be a witness to the mockers and hopefully a spirit of repentance hits their souls, and they escape a lake of fire for eternity.

3 False Christs

Matthew 24:5 for many shall come in my name, saying, I am Christ; and shall deceive many.

There are many false messiahs,' false prophets and other so called anointed people in the world today and has been through all history. I think most people know that Jesus last name was not Christ. First of all, the word "Christ" comes from christos, a Greek word meaning **"anointed."** It is the equivalent of the word mashiach, or Messiah, in Hebrew. So, to be the Christ, or Messiah, is to be "the anointed one of God." "JESUS ANOINTED OF GOD".

People all around the earth are claiming to be someone great and have this awesome anointing from God to do miracles or healings or other great feats of faith. Let these people blow wind long enough and then they quickly come up to the time where their true agenda lies, offering time where you the saints put piles of money into a bucket for them. I have heard them say God told them that there are a hundred people in the congregation who are supposed to put a thousand dollars each in the offering bucket. When asked if we could put in as much as we could afford, the anointed one sadly said I GUESS SO.

Being a new Christian and experiencing some of this really made me cautious. I remember going to a meeting where this preacher was supposed to be a witch hunter and cast out demons and be anointed to heal the sick. I went believing my little boy would get healed from a life-threatening medical situation. I took my son up for prayer and the anointed one prayed healing and declared he shall live and not die. He then grabbed me and prophesied loudly to the congregation that I had back problems and shoved me hard in the back and proclaimed healing over me and told me to sit down. I was totally fine, never had back problems but went out that night with a sore back from where he pushed very hard. A couple months later my son died in a foster care home. This man claimed to be someone he wasn't and have something he didn't. Another anointed one showed up and held a meeting in a hotel and when it was time to pray for folk this person stood up and acted like the power of God was flowing through his hands. I watched as each person he put his hands on fell to the floor. I was interested do I went up for prayer and when he came to me, he forcefully pushed on my forehead without saying any kind of prayer. The force of his push backwards made me lose my balance and fall to the floor. After he was done pushing folks over he then took up a huge offering doing the same speak as others. God said people were supposed to give a certain amount (100.00) dollars each because the power of God had knocked them down and ministered to them solving all their problems. These so-called Christ's or anointed ones rely on the spectacular rather than the supernatural to seduce people into thinking they are great ministers of God.

People today are hurting big time. Life has beaten them up and they are looking for help and love. The church has been so busy seeking fame and accolades that they turn a blind eye to the needs of humanity. So up from the masses of people arrives a charismatic individual that seems to have the right answers and a personality that draws hurting people. In the beginning all seems well until a God attitude surfaces. The spirit of Antichrist is that of **man making himself his own god**, that is, **man following his own will**. Satan's original sin was disobedience. The sin of Adam and Eve was disobedience. In the day in which we are living the Holy Spirit is emphasizing stern obedience to the Father.

Because the modern-day church is doing its own thing and not kingdom work opportunity is left for seducers flowing with the spirit of antichrist to bring destruction to human souls.

4 WARS TO UPHEAVELS IN THE EARTH

Matthew 24:6 and ye shall hear of wars and rumours of wars: see that ye be not troubled: for all *these things* must come to pass, but the end is not yet. 7 For nation shall rise against nation, and kingdom against kingdom: and there shall be famines, and pestilences, and earthquakes, in diver's places. 8 All these *are* the beginning of sorrows.

If you google wars in the earth today you will be shocked to find the earth is not a peaceful place. Wars have become so constant and active in the earth it is considered as common news and not worthy to report in order to get ratings. The sentence kingdoms against kingdoms refer to ethnic groups. Different Muslim denominations are at war with each other. Terrorist attacks all across the earth. Groups rebelling against their governments, trying to have a coup and oust the current government in order to get a dictatorship going are happening in multiple nations. The earth is not a safe place.

Famines

By Joe Hasell and Max Roser
https://ourworldindata.org/famines

First published in 2013; substantive revision December 7, 2017.

A famine is an acute episode of extreme hunger that results in excess mortality due to starvation. It is this crisis characteristic that distinguishes it from persistent malnutrition, which we discuss in another entry on this website. As we discuss in the Data Quality and Definition section below, the term 'famine' can mean different things to different people and has evolved over time. It is only in recent years that more precise, measurable definitions – in terms of mortality rates, food consumption and physical signs of malnutrition – have been developed.

But despite these ambiguities, it is nonetheless very clear that in recent decades the presence of major life-taking famines has diminished significantly and abruptly as compared to earlier eras. This is not in any way to underplay the very real risk facing the roughly 80 million people currently living in a state of crisis-level food insecurity and therefore requiring urgent action. Nevertheless, the parts of the world that continue to be at risk of famine represent a much more limited geographic area than in previous eras, and those famines that have occurred recently have typically been *far* less deadly – as we will go on to show in this entry.

For this entry we have assembled a new global dataset on famines from the 1860s until 2016. We estimate that in total 128 Million people died in famines over this period.

Famines have always occurred as the result of a complex mix of 'technical' and 'political' factors, but the developments of the modern industrial era have generally reduced the salience of natural constraints in causing famine. This includes many developments discussed in other pages of Our World in Data, such as the increasing availability of food per person, made possible through increasing agricultural yields; improvements in healthcare and sanitation; increased trade; reduced food prices and food price volatility; as well as reductions in the number of people living in extreme poverty. Over time, famines have become increasingly "man-made"-phenomena, becoming more clearly attributable to political causes, including non-democratic government and conflict. Paradoxically, over the course of the 20th century famine was virtually eradicated from most of the world, whilst over the same period there occurred some of the worst famines in recorded history. This is because many of the major famines of the 20th century were the outcome of wars or totalitarian regimes. As such, the waning of the very high levels of warfare over the last decades (as seen in the reduced number of battle deaths in recent times) and the spread of democratic institutions has also played a large part in the substantial reduction in famine mortality witnessed in recent decades.

Emergency food aid provided by relief agencies

continues to play a crucial role in preventing loss of life, and the international relief community has recently developed much better monitoring systems, such as the Famine Early Warning System, that has allowed for greater preparation and more timely interventions. Where poor harvests are the main cause of famine, as in Niger in 2005, relief provision tends to prevent marked increases in mortality. It is the presence of conflict, or abuses of political power that can block food supplies reaching populations which represents the most pertinent trigger of 'death-dealing' famines today.

Thus, overall, we can see in the rapid decline of famine mortality one of the great accomplishments of our era, representing technological progress, economic development and the spread of stable democracies. Viewed in this light, however, it also serves to highlight the appalling continued presence of famines which are, in the modern world, entirely man-made.

Pestilence

Noun

pes·ti·lence | \ ˈpe-stə-lən(t)s \

Definition of *pestilence*

1 : a contagious or infectious epidemic disease that is virulent and devastating *especially* : BUBONIC PLAGUE

2 : something that is destructive or pernicious

Disease outbreaks and epidemics are commonplace throughout the world. Ranging from seasonal flu to the world-wide spread of HIV Aids and the latest pandemic of covid 19. The effects of disease outbreaks often remain hidden in the recesses of our minds until they hit home. History has seen its fair share of life-altering disease outbreaks and pandemics. Is the 21st Century prone to another pandemic? With a growing healthcare infrastructure in the world today, are global epidemics even possible? Or can a disease found in a third-world country bring a nation like a modern technological nation to its knees? The answer is a profound yes, and its reasoning may surprise many.

Several disease outbreaks and epidemics throughout history have crippled nations and even the world. The following are ten disease epidemics that have the potential to do the same in the world today, both as healthcare and socio-economic crises: https://www.realworldsurvivor.com/2018/03/16/top-10-epidemics/

Tuberculosis

Tuberculosis (TB) is an infectious disease caused by bacteria that mainly affects the lungs. It has been prevalent even during ancient times. During the 18th Century, some believed that tuberculosis was attributed to vampires, since many in a family would slowly become ill after the death of one family member. During the early 20th Century, tuberculosis was responsible for one in six deaths in France and was associated with those living in urban poverty.

TB is an airborne disease spread through coughing and sneezing. Although almost one-third of the world's population is believed to be infected with tuberculosis, it's prevalence in slowly declining through better healthcare efforts. It remains one of the epidemics with widespread public health effects in developing countries. This resulted in almost 1.5 million deaths in 2014. Those living in highly populated and poverty-stricken regions are often affected with tuberculosis, which has an estimated 22 percent infection rate. Because TB is the second-most common cause of death among infectious diseases (second to HIV/AIDS), it remains an epidemic that can adversely affect our world's safety today.

Dengue Fever

Dengue fever is a mosquito-borne tropical disease caused by the dengue virus. Symptoms resemble most other flu-like symptoms with a characteristic skin rash. However, some symptoms develop into Dengue hemorrhagic fever which can result in bleeding, low blood platelets, and shock when blood pressure falls to dangerous levels.

There is a vaccine for Dengue Fever, although its use is minimal as it is only 60 percent effective.

Marburg Virus

The Marburg virus disease (MVD) was first identified in 1967 during epidemics in Marburg Germany through infected research monkeys delivered from Uganda. MVD is a severe and highly fatal disease caused by a virus from the same family as Ebola. It is among the most virulent pathogens known to mankind. Symptoms begin abruptly with severe headaches, which often lead to hemorrhagic fevers less than a week later. Fatalities are often accompanied by severe bleeding from the body's orifices, especially through projectile vomit and explosive diarrhea. Fatality rates range anywhere between 25 percent from the 1967 outbreak to more than 80 percent in later outbreaks seen between 1998 and 2005.

Like similar viruses, the Marburg virus is transmitted by direct contact with the bodily fluids of infected persons, or by handling dead infected wild animals. The virus originates from African fruit bats, where it remains endemic in African nations today. Although lesser known, an outbreak could mean widespread disease in underdeveloped regions.

Malaria

Malaria is a parasite that is transmitted through a species of mosquito known as Anopheles. It causes severe illness in those infected with the disease. According to the World Health Organization (WHO), over 3.2 billion people live in regions endemic with the disease. This is responsible for over 212 million cases of illness in 2015 that resulted in 429,000 deaths. Severe Malaria symptoms are complicated by serious organ failure, impairment of consciousness, seizures, coma, and death if left untreated.

Although Malaria was all but eliminated in the United States in the early 1950s, there are almost 2,000 cases reported each year. These are mostly from travelers that bring the disease into the nation's borders. Because the United States is home to the Anopheles mosquito, the mosquito species responsible for carrying Malaria, there is always a risk that Malaria could make a comeback.

Plague

No disease in the history of mankind has the diabolical stigma that Plague does. "Plague" is often used to reference our greatest fears in the world of epidemics. Technically, the Plague is an infectious disease that is caused by the bacterium *Yersinia pestis.* It is which is transmitted through fleas after feeding off infected rats. Once the Plague finds a host in the human body, it will manifest itself in one of three different forms: Bubonic, Septicemic, and the deadliest form, Pneumonic. Once in these forms, the Plague is spreadable in the air or through direct contact to others.

All but eradicated in developed countries, Plague still rears its ugly head in pockets throughout the world. It remains a concern for public health disease specialists. Plague is highly contagious, extremely vicious, and could cause death within the same day if left untreated. Although Plague is not a prevalent disease in the world today. The fact that it has such a high fatality rate, it has adversely altered the socio-economic landscapes of history's most powerful nations. As well, it has been used effectively as a bio-terrorism agent throughout time. It is considered one of the most dangerous diseases known to man. Is it likely to resurface as another pandemic? If it does, however, you can bet that the world as seen today would be forever marred by its deadly clutches.

SARS

Ebola Experts Clear Up Rumors about Virus

SARS, or Severe Acute Respiratory Syndrome, saw its first and only outbreak between 2002 and 2003. It is a respiratory disease that is caused by a coronavirus. During its outbreak, which started in Southern China and spread to 37 countries, SARS infected almost 8,100 individuals. Of which

774 died from the infection.

A case of SARS hasn't been reported since 2004, which is lucky because it has a 9.6 percent fatality rate. Its symptoms are flu-like, but eventually can lead to viral or bacterial pneumonia. With no known vaccine, the only effective means of containment is isolation, quarantine, and personal hygiene.

SARS left the world as mysteriously as it swept in with no known cause or vaccine to combat it. Although public health efforts worked, it remains a bleak reminder that nature is in control.

Cholera

Cholera is a disease that has been the by-product of most wars and natural disasters throughout history. It is caused by a bacterial infection within the intestines that develops massive amounts of fluid in the intestinal cells. This leads to explosive vomiting and diarrhea. The infection spreads through contaminated food and water that has traces of vomit or feces. This causes massive outbreaks in short amounts of time through overcrowded areas that lack clean water and basic sanitation systems. Recent Cholera outbreaks have been seen in the Haiti Earthquake of 2010, and war-torn areas such as Yemen and Syria.

Symptoms of Cholera appear within three days and result from severe dehydration due to the profuse vomiting and diarrhea. Without treatment, patients may die within hours.

According to the WHO, Cholera affects 1.4 to 4.3 million people worldwide. It is responsible from anywhere between 28,000 to 142,000 deaths per year. There have been six Cholera pandemics in history that are responsible for millions of deaths worldwide. A current pandemic began in South Asia in 1961 which spread to the Americas in 1991, where it remains an endemic disease today.

Ebola

No epidemics have affected the media like the 2015 Ebola epidemic in West Africa. This is history's largest recorded outbreak. It included almost 11,500 deaths, including one American. The last Ebola outbreak is a grim reminder that diseases not only affect the healthcare status in countries, but also socio-economic and emotional psyches as well. Ebola is a hemorrhagic disease from the Filoviridae virus family that causes severe hemorrhaging from orifices such as the mouth, anus, and nose.

It was first discovered in 1976 near the Ebola River in Africa and has since then spread through communal pockets within the continent. The natural carrier of Ebola remains a mystery. Many health officials believe that the virus is an animal-borne disease found in bats. Most individuals get Ebola through direct contract of bodily fluids such as urine, saliva, sweat, feces, vomit, breast milk, and semen. Can Ebola become a fast-growing epidemic here in America?

The 2015 Ebola scare in America creates a healthy debate of which can be worse: the disease outbreak itself, or the consequence that lead to changes in a nation's governmental response. Ebola is an extremely frightening disease that has no cure.

The fact that its victims die an excruciatingly painful and grotesque death heighten the fear. Ebola is highly contagious, especially in third world countries and healthcare settings. What is the safest way to stay safe from Ebola? Stay far, far away from it.

Zika

The Zika virus is an interesting disease in that it does not pose a substantial health risk to those who contract it. It does, however, pose a serious risk to unborn children who, if infected with Zika, may develop a condition known as Microcephaly. This causes severe brain damage and is manifest as an infant's abnormally small head-to-body ratio size. Nature is in Control

Disease outbreaks and epidemics are no different

and bear the grim reminder that human life is fragile and that ultimately, nature is in control. Epidemics experts can readily track disease outbreaks, and hopefully stop the spread of disease before it gets out of hand. But past our technology and extensive medical expertise, history tells us another story in which nature occasionally reminds us that it is in charge, that silent organisms exist that have leveled societies, and we are often bystanders to stand in awe of their veracity. Although silent disasters wait to reveal themselves, it is our job to learn from history's worst epidemics, prepare our families as best possible, but also live life to the fullest in light of what will eventually be.

Today's Earthquakes

*https://***earthquaketrack.com***/recent*

190 **earthquakes** in the past 24 hours. 1,274 **earthquakes** in the past 7 days. 4,967 **earthquakes** in the past 30 days. 64,181 **earthquakes** in the past 365 days. This was as of April 9, 2020. You can look at the link above and get updated information. In today's tech advanced world, you can most information via the internet. Our world is becoming smaller. We are able to communicate with someone on the other side of the planet with the click of a button.

Convergence

Many people will say we have always had plagues famines and earthquakes. That may be true but when you research history it will be one here, one there and decades apart. An earthquake in this century, a famine in this decade and pestilence in this millennium. They were separate and far apart. As we get closer to the time of the gentiles being fulfilled Luke 21:24. I believe the time of the gentiles is now when God is dealing with the gentile nations. That is all nations that are not of the nation of Israel. God's desire is that all mankind be saved, and he knows who will accept Jesus as savior and Lord of their lives. God knows when, who, and everyone's name throughout eternity. Only God the Father knows how many people will complete the body of Christ. He has allotted a certain amount of time for that goal to be accomplished and it shall. As we see the signs leading to that fulfillment Jesus told His Israeli followers that the end is not yet but Matthew 24:**8** all these *are* the beginning of sorrows. The term sorrows here are also translated birth pangs in other translations. These events are more serious and more often. They do not come individually and once in a long time anymore, but they appear together and more intense and more often than before. Just like a woman giving birth to a child.

Present Suffering and Future Glory

Romans 8:18 I consider that our present sufferings
are not worth comparing with the glory that will
be revealed in us. **19** For the creation waits in
eager expectation for the children of God to be
revealed. **20** For the creation was subjected to
frustration, not by its own choice, but by the will
of the one who subjected it, in hope **21** that the
creation itself will be liberated from its bondage
to decay and brought into the freedom and glory
of the children of God. **22** We know that the whole
creation has been groaning as in the pains of
childbirth right up to the present time. **23** Not only
so, but we ourselves, who have the first fruits of
the Spirit, groan inwardly as we wait eagerly for
our adoption to son ship, the redemption of our

bodies. 24 For in this hope we were saved. But
hope that is seen is no hope at all. Who hopes for
what they already have? 25 But if we hope for
what we do not yet have, we wait for it patiently.

26 In the same way, the Spirit helps us in our
weakness. We do not know what we ought to
pray for, but the Spirit himself intercedes for us
through wordless groans. 27 And he who searches
our hearts knows the mind of the Spirit, because
the Spirit intercedes for God's people in
accordance with the will of God.

28 And we know that in all things God works for
the good of those who love him, who have been
called according to his purpose. 29 For those God
foreknew he also predestined to be conformed to
the image of his Son, that he might be the
firstborn among many brothers and sisters.
30 And those he predestined, he also called; those
he called, he also justified; those he justified, he
also glorified.

All the earthquakes, wars, pestilences, famines and other stressful events in the earth are in actuality birth pains.

Romans 8:22 New International Version

we know that the whole creation has been groaning as in the pains of childbirth right up to the present time.

The question you have to ask is what is creation trying to birth? I believe 1 Corinthians 15 gives us the answer.

1 Corinthians 15 New King James Version (NKJV)

The Risen Christ, Faith's Reality

15 Moreover, brethren, I declare to you the
gospel which I preached to you, which also you
received and in which you stand, [2] by which also
you are saved, if you hold fast that word which I
preached to you—unless you believed in vain.

[3] For I delivered to you first of all that which I also
received: that Christ died for our sins according
to the Scriptures, [4] and that He was buried, and
that He rose again the third day according to the

Scriptures, [5] and that He was seen by Cephas,
then by the twelve. [6] After that He was seen by
over five hundred brethren at once, of whom the
greater part remain to the present, but some
have fallen asleep. [7] After that He was seen by
James, then by all the apostles. [8] Then last of all
He was seen by me also, as by one born out of
due time.

[9] For I am the least of the apostles, who am not
worthy to be called an apostle, because I
persecuted the church of God. [10] But by the grace
of God I am what I am, and His grace toward me
was not in vain; but I labored more abundantly
than they all, yet not I, but the grace of God
which was with me. [11] Therefore, whether *it was* I
or they, so we preach and so you believed.

The Risen Christ, Our Hope

[12] Now if Christ is preached that He has been
raised from the dead, how do some among you
say that there is no resurrection of the dead?
[13] But if there is no resurrection of the dead, then
Christ is not risen. [14] And if Christ is not risen,

then our preaching *is* empty, and your faith *is*
also empty. [15] Yes, and we are found false
witnesses of God, because we have testified of
God that He raised up Christ, whom He did not
raise up—if in fact the dead do not rise. [16] For if
the dead do not rise, then Christ is not risen.
[17] And if Christ is not risen, your faith *is* futile; you
are still in your sins! [18] Then also those who have
fallen asleep in Christ have perished. [19] If in this
life only we have hope in Christ, we are of all men
the most pitiable.

The Last Enemy Destroyed

[20] But now Christ is risen from the dead and has
become the first fruits of those who have fallen
asleep. [21] For since by man *came* death, by Man
also *came* the resurrection of the dead. [22] For as
in Adam all die, even so in Christ all shall be made
alive. [23] But each one in his own order: Christ the
first fruits, afterward those *who are* Christ's at His
coming. [24] Then *comes* the end, when He delivers
the kingdom to God the Father, when He puts an
end to all rule and all authority and power. [25] For
He must reign till He has put all enemies under

His feet. 26 The last enemy *that* will be destroyed
is death. 27 For "He has put all things under His
feet." But when He says, "all things are put under
Him," it is evident that He who put all things
under Him is accepted. 28 Now when all things are
made subject to Him, then the Son Himself will
also be subject to Him who put all things under
Him that God may be all in all.

Effects of Denying the Resurrection

29 Otherwise, what will they do who are baptized
for the dead, if the dead do not rise at all? Why
then are they baptized for the dead? 30 And why
do we stand in jeopardy every hour? 31 I affirm,
by the boasting in you whom I have in Christ
Jesus our Lord, I die daily. 32 If, in the manner of
men, I have fought with beasts at Ephesus, what
advantage *is it* to me? If *the* dead do not rise,
"Let us eat and drink, for tomorrow we die!"

33 Do not be deceived: "Evil Company corrupts
good habits." 34 Awake to righteousness, and do
not sin; for some do not have the knowledge of
God. I speak *this* to your shame.

A Glorious Body

[35] But someone will say, "How are the dead raised
up? And with what body do they come?"
[36] Foolish one, what you sow is not made alive
unless it dies. [37] And what you sow, you do not
sow that body that shall be, but mere grain
perhaps wheat or some other *grain.* [38] But God
gives it a body as He pleases, and to each seed its
own body.

[39] All flesh *is* not the same flesh, but *there is* one
kind of flesh of men, another flesh of animals,
another of fish, *and* another of birds.

[40] *There are* also celestial bodies and terrestrial
bodies; but the glory of the celestial *is* one, and
the *glory* of the terrestrial *is* another. [41] *There is*
one glory of the sun, another glory of the moon,
and another glory of the stars; for *one* star differs
from *another* star in glory.

[42] So also *is* the resurrection of the dead. *The*
body is sown in corruption, it is raised in
incorrupt ion. [43] It is sown in dishonor; it is raised
in glory. It is sown in weakness; it is raised in

power. 44 It is sown as a natural body; it is raised a spiritual body. There is a natural body, and there is a spiritual body. 45 And so it is written, "The first man Adam became a living being." The last Adam *became* a life-giving spirit.

46 However, the spiritual is not first, but the natural, and afterward the spiritual. 47 The first man *was* of the earth, *made* of dust; the second Man *is* the Lord from heaven. 48 As *was* the *man* of dust, so also *are* those *who are made* of dust; and as *is* the heavenly *Man,* so also *are* those *who are* heavenly. 49 And as we have borne the image of the *man* of dust, we shall also bear the image of the heavenly *Man.*

Our Final Victory

50 Now this I say, brethren, that flesh and blood cannot inherit the kingdom of God; nor does corruption inherit incorrupt ion. 51 Behold, I tell you a mystery: We shall not all sleep, but we shall all be changed 52 in a moment, in the twinkling of an eye, at the last trumpet. For the trumpet will sound, and the dead will be raised incorruptible,

and we shall be changed. [53] For this corruptible
must put on incorrupt ion, and this mortal *must*
put on immortality. [54] So when this corruptible
has put on incorrupt ion, and this mortal has put on immortality, then shall be brought to pass the saying that is written: "Death is swallowed up in victory."

[55] "O Death, where *is* your sting?
O Hades, where *is* your victory?"

[56] The sting of death *is* sin, and the strength of sin
is the law. [57] But thanks *be* to God, who gives us
the victory through our Lord Jesus Christ.

[58] Therefore, my beloved brethren, be steadfast, immovable, always abounding in the work of the Lord, knowing that your labor is not in vain in the Lord.

If these times and troubles are birth pains we should be in constant communication with the Holy Spirit.

5 WITNESSING TO ALL NATIONS

Witnessing to All Nations

(Mark 13:10-13; Luke 21:10-19)

9 Then shall they deliver you up to be afflicted,
and shall kill you: and ye shall be hated of all
nations for my name's sake. **10** And then shall
many be offended, and shall betray one another,
and shall hate one another. **11** And many false
prophets shall rise, and shall deceive many. **12**
And because iniquity shall abound, the love of
many shall wax cold. **13** But he that shall endure
unto the end, the same shall be saved. **14** And
this gospel of the kingdom shall be preached in
the entire world for a witness unto all nations;
and then shall the end come.

We are seeing a rise in Christians being persecuted. Jailed, tortured, and even put to death for their faith in Jesus Christ. However, in the same respect the Gospel of salvation in the Lord Jesus Christ is preached throughout the entire earth.

Extraordinary stories about the massive number of Muslims converting to Christianity are appearing around the world. Recently at World Magazine, writer Warren Cole Smith interviewed 25-year missionary David Garrison who has documented his findings about the Muslim phenomenon. "There is a revival in the Muslim world," Garrison says. He believes between 2 and 7 million former Muslims have converted to Christianity in the past two decades. His book, *A Wind in the House of Islam,* contains impressive research to back up his claim.

China's on track to contain the world's largest Christian population thanks to a surge in underground house churches and state-sanction places of worship, according to the Council of Foreign Relations.

In a background document titled "Christianity in

China," the CFR estimates of the number of Protestants at anywhere from 58 million to 115 million and higher — though fewer than 30 million attend officially registered churches.

You can search the internet and find millions of people religious, cultural, and nationwide converting to Jesus. People are hurting and disillusioned with their religion, philosophy, and life in general. Jesus Christ is the only source of stability in this dark confusing world. The world is growing dark. With each birth pain or crisis, catastrophe hope seems to be fading rapidly.

Isaiah 60:2 [2]See, darkness covers the earth and thick darkness is over the peoples, but the LORD rises upon you and his glory appears over you.

Read Isaiah 60:2 Using Other Translations

KJV

For, behold, the darkness shall cover the earth, and gross darkness the people: but the LORD shall arise upon thee, and his glory shall be seen upon thee.

ESV

For behold, darkness shall cover the earth, and thick darkness the peoples; but the LORD will arise upon you and his glory will be seen upon you.

NLT

Darkness as black as night covers all the nations of the earth, but the glory of the LORD rises and appears over you.

It is very obvious that darkness is covering the earth and question to you believer is, are you in a position with Christ to allow His Glory to manifest Himself through you and be a source of light in a dark world?

Mark 16:15-19 New International Version (NIV)

15 He said to them, "Go into all the world and
preach the gospel to all creation. **16** Whoever

believes and is baptized will be saved, but
whoever does not believe will be condemned.
17 And these signs will accompany those who
believe: In my name they will drive out demons;
they will speak in new tongues; **18** they will pick
up snakes with their hands; and when they drink
deadly poison, it will not hurt them at all; they
will place their hands on sick people, and they
will get well."

19 After the Lord Jesus had spoken to them, he
was taken up into heaven and he sat at the right
hand of God.

This verse gives you authority to act as an ambassador of Jesus.

2 Corinthians 5:17–21

The New King James Version

17 Therefore, if anyone *is* in Christ, *he is* a new creation; old things have passed away; behold, all things have become new. 18 Now all things *are* of God, who has reconciled us to Himself through Jesus Christ, and has given us the ministry of

reconciliation, 19 that is, that God was in Christ reconciling the world to Himself, not imputing their trespasses to them, and has committed to us the word of reconciliation.

20 Now then, we are ambassadors for Christ, as though God were pleading through us: we implore *you* on Christ's behalf, be reconciled to God. 21 For He made Him who knew no sin *to be* sin for us, that we might become the righteousness of God in Him.

Crazy times are definitely here; you can cruise the internet and find a wide variety of Christians believing a wide variety of winds of doctrines. One of the ones I get amused at is We are in the book of revelation and experiencing seal number? They chose 1900 as marker and then start declaring past events like world war one as a certain seal and carried up to the present generation. The book of revelation covers a seven-year gap not a seven-hundred-year time frame. So, after listening to this nonsense, I chuckle and ask the Holy Spirit to guide me in all things and reveal truth and light to me.

If we are in the book of revelation we are in chapters 1-3.

Revelation1 (NKJV)

Introduction and Benediction

1 The Revelation of Jesus Christ, which God gave Him to show His servants—things which must shortly take place. And He sent and signified *it* by His angel to His servant John, [2] who bore witness to the word of God, and to the testimony of Jesus Christ, to all things that he saw. [3] Blessed *is* he who reads and those who hear the words of this prophecy, and keep those things which are written in it; for the time *is* near.

Greeting the Seven Churches

[4] John, to the seven churches which are in Asia:

Grace to you and peace from Him who is and who was and who is to come, and from the seven Spirits who are before His throne, [5] and from Jesus Christ, the faithful witness, the firstborn

from the dead, and the ruler over the kings of the
earth.

To Him who]loved us and washed us from our
sins in His own blood, 6 and has made us kings
and priests to His God and Father, to Him *be*
glory and dominion forever and ever. Amen.

7 Behold, He is coming with clouds, and every eye
will see Him, even they who pierced Him. And all
the tribes of the earth will mourn because of
Him. Even so, Amen.

8 "I am the Alpha and the Omega, *the* Beginning
and *the* End," says the Lord, "who is and who was
and who is to come, the Almighty."

Vision of the Son of Man

9 I, John, both your brother and companion in the
tribulation and kingdom and patience of Jesus
Christ, was on the island that is called Patmos for
the word of God and for the testimony of Jesus
Christ. 10 I was in the Spirit on the Lord's Day, and
I heard behind me a loud voice, as of a trumpet,
11 saying, "I am the Alpha and the Omega, the

First and the Last," and, "What you see, write in a
book and send *it* to the seven churches which are
in Asia: to Ephesus, to Smyrna, to Pergamos, to
Thyatira, to Sardis, to Philadelphia, and to
Laodicea."

12 Then I turned to see the voice that spoke with
me. And having turned I saw seven golden
lampstands, 13 and in the midst of the seven
lampstands *One* like the Son of Man, clothed with
a garment down to the feet and girded about the
chest with a golden band. 14 His head and hair
were white like wool, as white as snow, and His
eyes like a flame of fire; 15 His feet *were* like fine
brass, as if refined in a furnace, and His voice as
the sound of many waters; 16 He had in His right
hand seven stars, out of His mouth went a sharp
two-edged sword, and His countenance *was* like
the sun shining in its strength. 17 And when I saw
Him, I fell at His feet as dead. But He laid His right
hand on me, saying to me, "Do not be afraid; I am
the First and the Last. 18 I *am* He who lives, and
was dead, and behold, I am alive forevermore.
Amen. And I have the keys of Hades and of

Death. [19] Write the things which you have seen, and the things which are, and the things which will take place after this. [20] The mystery of the seven stars which you saw in My right hand, and the seven golden lampstands: The seven stars are the angels of the seven churches, and the seven lampstands which you saw are the seven churches.

Revelation 2 New King James Version (NKJV)

The Loveless Church

2 "To the angel of the church of Ephesus write,

'These things says He who holds the seven stars in His right hand, who walks in the midst of the seven golden lampstands: [2] "I know your works, your labor, your patience, and that you cannot bear those who are evil. And you have tested those who say they are apostles and are not, and have found them liars; [3] and you have persevered and have patience, and have labored for My name's sake and have not become weary. [4] Nevertheless I have *this* against you, that you have left your first love. [5] Remember therefore

from where you have fallen; repent and do the
first works, or else I will come to you quickly and
remove your lampstand from its place unless you
repent. 6 But this you have, that you hate the
deeds of the Nicolaitans, which I also hate.

7 "He who has an ear, let him hear what the Spirit
says to the churches. To him who overcomes I
will give to eat from the tree of life, which is in
the midst of the Paradise of God." '

The Persecuted Church

8 "And to the angel of the church in Smyrna write,

'These things says the First and the Last, who was
dead, and came to life: 9 "I know your works,
tribulation, and poverty (but you are rich); and *I
know* the blasphemy of those who say they are
Jews and are not, but *are* a synagogue of Satan.
10 Do not fear any of those things which you are
about to suffer. Indeed, the devil is about to
throw *some* of you into prison, that you may be
tested, and you will have tribulation ten days. Be
faithful until death, and I will give you the crown
of life.

[11] "He who has an ear, let him hear what the Spirit says to the churches. He who overcomes shall not be hurt by the second death." '

The Compromising Church

[12] "And to the angel of the church in Pergamos write,

'These things says He who has the sharp two-
edged sword: [13] "I know your works, and where
you dwell, where Satan's throne *is.* And you hold
fast to My name, and did not deny My faith even
in the days in which Antipas *was* My faithful
martyr, who was killed among you, where Satan
dwells. [14] But I have a few things against you,
because you have there those who hold the
doctrine of Balaam, who taught Balak to put a
stumbling block before the children of Israel, to
eat things sacrificed to idols, and to commit
sexual immorality. [15] Thus you also have those
who hold the doctrine of the Nicolaitans, which
thing I hate. [16] Repent, or else I will come to you
quickly and will fight against them with the sword
of My mouth.

[17] "He who has an ear, let him hear what the
Spirit says to the churches. To him who
overcomes I will give some of the hidden manna
to eat. And I will give him a white stone, and on
the stone a new name written which no one
knows except him who receives *it.*" '

The Corrupt Church

[18] "And to the angel of the church in Thyatira
write,

'These things says the Son of God, who has eyes
like a flame of fire, and His feet like fine brass:
[19] "I know your works, love, service, faith, and
your patience; and *as* for your works, the last *are*
more than the first. [20] Nevertheless I have a few
things against you, because you allow that
woman Jezebel, who calls herself a prophetess,
to teach and seduce My servants to commit
sexual immorality and eat things sacrificed to
idols. [21] And I gave her time to repent of her
sexual immorality, and she did not repent.
[22] Indeed I will cast her into a sickbed, and those
who commit adultery with her into great

tribulation, unless they repent of their deeds. [23] I
will kill her children with death, and all the
churches shall know that I am He who searches
the minds and hearts. And I will give to each one
of you according to your works.

[24] "Now to you I say, and to the rest in Thyatira,
as many as do not have this doctrine, who have
not known the depths of Satan, as they say, I will
put on you no other burden. [25] But hold fast what
you have till I come. [26] And he who overcomes,
and keeps My works until the end, to him I will
give power over the nations.

[27] 'He shall rule them with a rod of iron;
They shall be dashed to pieces like the potter's
vessels'—

as I also have received from My Father; [28,] and I
will give him the morning star.

[29] "He who has an ear, let him hear what the
Spirit says to the churches." '

Revelation 3 New King James Version (NKJV)

The Dead Church

3 "And to the angel of the church in Sardis write,

'These things says He who has the seven Spirits of
God and the seven stars: "I know your works,
that you have a name that you are alive, but you
are dead. [2] Be watchful, and strengthen the
things which remain, that are ready to die, for I
have not found your works perfect before God.
[3] Remember therefore how you have received
and heard; hold fast and repent. Therefore, if you
do not watch, I will come upon you as a thief, and
you will not know what hour I will come upon
you. [4] You have a few names even in Sardis who
have not defiled their garments; and they shall
walk with Me in white, for they are worthy. [5] He
who overcomes shall be clothed in white
garments, and I will not blot out his name from
the Book of Life; but I will confess his name
before My Father and before His angels.

[6] "He who has an ear, let him hear what the Spirit
says to the churches." '

The Faithful Church

7 "And to the angel of the church in Philadelphia
write,

'These things says He who is holy, He who is true,
"He who has the key of David, He who opens, and
no one shuts, and shuts and no one opens": 8 "I
know your works. See, I have set before you an
open door, and no one can shut it; for you have a
little strength, have kept My word, and have not
denied My name. 9 Indeed I will make *those* of
the synagogue of Satan, who say they are Jews
and are not, but lie indeed I will make them come
and worship before your feet, and to know that I
have loved you. 10 Because you have kept My
command to persevere, I also will keep you from
the hour of trial which shall come upon the whole
world, to test those who dwell on the earth.
11 Behold, I am coming quickly! Hold fast what
you have, that no one may take your crown. 12 He
who overcomes, I will make him a pillar in the
temple of My God, and he shall go out no more. I
will write on him the name of My God and the
name of the city of My God, the New Jerusalem,
which comes down out of heaven from My God.

And *I will write on him* My new name.

[13] "He who has an ear, let him hear what the
Spirit says to the churches." '

The Lukewarm Church

[14] "And to the angel of the church of the
Laodiceans write,

'These things says the Amen, the Faithful and
True Witness, the Beginning of the creation of
God: **15** "I know your works, that you are neither
cold nor hot. I wish you were cold or hot. **16** So
then, because you are lukewarm, and neither
cold nor hot, I will vomit you out of My mouth.
17 Because you say, 'I am rich, have become
wealthy, and have need of nothing'—and do not
know that you are wretched, miserable, poor,
blind, and naked— **18** I counsel you to buy from
Me gold refined in the fire, that you may be rich;
and white garments, that you may be clothed,
that the shame of your nakedness may not be
revealed; and anoint your eyes with eye salve,
that you may see. **19** As many as I love, I rebuke
and chasten. Therefore, be zealous and repent.

20 Behold, I stand at the door and knock. If
anyone hears My voice and opens the door, I will
come into him and dine with him, and he with
Me. **21** To him who overcomes I will grant to sit
with Me on My throne, as I also overcame and
sat down with My Father on His throne.

22 "He who has an ear, let him hear what the
Spirit says to the churches."

You can see evidence of every kind of theses churches in the earth today. Each that overcomes has a promise from the Lord Jesus Christ. One church I have always been curious about is the church of Philadelphia. **The Faithful Church**

7 "And to the angel of the church in Philadelphia
write,

'These things says He who is holy, He who is true,
"He who has the key of David, He who opens, and
no one shuts, and shuts and no one opens": **8** "I
know your works. See, I have set before you an

open door, and no one can shut it; for you have a
little strength, have kept My word, and have not
denied My name. [9] Indeed I will make *those* of
the synagogue of Satan, who say they are Jews
and are not, but lie indeed I will make them come
and worship before your feet, and to know that I
have loved you. [10] Because you have kept My
command to persevere, I also will keep you from
the hour of trial which shall come upon the whole
world, to test those who dwell on the earth.
[11] Behold, I am coming quickly! Hold fast what
you have, that no one may take your crown. [12] He
who overcomes, I will make him a pillar in the
temple of My God, and he shall go out no more. I
will write on him the name of My God and the
name of the city of My God, the New Jerusalem,
which comes down out of heaven from My God.
And *I will write on him* My new name.

[13] "He who has an ear, let him hear what the
Spirit says to the churches." '

One verse in particular, [10] Because you have kept My command to persevere, I also will keep you from the hour of trial which shall come upon

the whole world, to test those who dwell on the earth. Besides the pandemic being a birth pain, even though God never inflicted the earth with such virus, perchance He is taking something Satan used man to create as a tool to test all that dwell on the earth. Non-Christian and Christian alike you will be tested in this situation to see your belief system and faith. Unbelievers will do what is in their nature, respond through fear and act accordingly. Believer are you going to mimic the world or Because you have kept My command to persevere, I also will keep you from the hour of trial which shall come upon the whole world, to test those who dwell on the earth. Walk in fellowship with the Holy Spirit and trust Him to protect you through this situation and every situation. I believe we are experiencing a convergence of birth pains and testing. This convergence makes verse 11-13 real and
imminent **11** Behold, I am coming quickly! Hold
fast what you have, that no one may take your
crown. **12** He who overcomes, I will make him a
pillar in the temple of My God, and he shall go
out no more. I will write on him the name of My

God and the name of the city of My God, the New Jerusalem, which comes down out of heaven from My God. And *I will write on him* My new name.

[13] "He who has an ear, let him hear what the Spirit says to the churches." '

When you look at verse 9 . [9] Indeed I will make *those* of the synagogue of Satan, who say they are Jews and are not, but lie—indeed I will make them come and worship before your feet, and to know that I have loved you. This verse in essence says we are ambassadors. Each nation has ambassadors that basically bow in respect to the authority of the nations they are in representing their home country.

Philippians 3:20 **New King James Version**
For our citizenship is in heaven, from which we also eagerly wait for the Savior, the Lord Jesus Christ,

Heaven is our home country and 2 Corinthians 5:20 says we are ambassadors representing Christ. We operate in the earth with the authority of heaven behind us. Not only did Jesus give us His authority but we have the power of heaven backing the authority.

We are in a movement of holiness throughout the earth. This is evident by Donald Trump getting into office in the United States and Rodrigo Duterte becoming president in the Philippines. God usually puts signs in the earth where people can see them, not necessarily understand them, but there to signify a move of the Spirit. Both presidents have made it a priority to clean up their individual nations. Trump to clean the swamp a title he has given the government. Duterte cleaning up drug dealers and corrupt police and politicians throughout the nation. The Philippines has a reputation of being one of the most corrupt nations in the earth today. One word hated by a lot of people is repent even in the church today. Church leaders who have a brief case of good works to present to Jesus at the bema seat forget that they are not giving account of themselves to their denomination heads who think their works are great. They think they are great and deserve the respect of all in their organization by calling them by the titles they gave themselves. They want to hear ooooohhhh dr. big wig enter the building try to have a glazed look of awe and wonderment in your eyes when he passes by. Sure, they may have done good works. Are they building their own empires in order for men to build up their egos. How many denominations and churches are into empire building to get famous, finances and a big ego? Building the kingdom of God in the earth and not seeking recognition or wealth from men for your efforts will stand at the bema seat of Christ. To build the kingdom of God you have to follow the instructions of the master builder the Holy Spirit. Not only follow but yield yourself to the Holy Spirit completely and let Him flow through you and do the work through you and for you. You yielded to the Holy Spirit because you could see no way to do what He asked. You yielded out of love for Him. He moved in you fulfilled His instructions through you and at the bema seat you get the reward as if you did it when all you did was give your entire self into the hands of the Holy Spirit not my will, but your will be done.

Mark 14:36: And he said, "Abba, Father, all things are possible for you. Remove this cup from me. Yet not what I will, but what you will." (ESV)

Luke 22:42: "Father, if you are willing, take this cup from me; yet not my will, but yours be done." (NIV)

You used Jesus example as your guideline in life. In these last days staying close and hearing and obeying the Holy Spirit is crucial. Repentance before resurrection, be a clean vessel and let us throw off all hindrances **Hebrews 12:1-3**
1Therefore, since we are surrounded by such a great cloud of witnesses, let us throw off everything **that hinders** and the sin that so easily entangles. And let us run with perseverance the
race marked out for us, 2fixing our eyes on Jesus, the pioneer and perfecter of faith. For the joy set before him he endured the cross, scorning its shame, and sat down at the right hand of the
throne of God. 3Consider him who endured such

opposition from sinners, so that you will not grow weary and lose heart.

6 THE END IS NEAR

Bible prophecies that are on the verge of being fulfilled which signify the upcoming events of the book of revelation strike a sense of excitement in my heart. Not because of the dread or chaos of the prophecy but what may come before the prophetic event. Jeremiah 49:23-27 and Isaiah 17:1 *Proclamation Against Syria and Israel*

17 The burden against Damascus.

"Behold, Damascus will cease from *being* a city,

And it will be a ruinous heap.

Damascus may have been conquered in the past but never completely destroyed to become a ruinous heap. That kind of destruction comes through atomic warfare. Also, Ezekiel 38-39 which talks about outlying nations joining together to take a plunder from Israel. These two events are on the verge of happening. In Ezekiel 38-39 God goes to war defending Israel. No other nation helps just make a weak criticizing remark.

Now if God is going to war in the earth is it the start of the book of revelation where Jesus is revealed as king and saves Israel and fights against all evil and unbelievers in the earth. If this is the case when a country declares war on another country the first thing they do is call their ambassadors home. All the nations seem to be lined up and ready for action. Perchance we are about to experience **Revelation 4:1** [1]After this I looked, and there before me was a door standing open in heaven. And the voice I had first heard speaking to me like a trumpet said, "Come up here, and I will show you what must take place after this."

The apostle John is symbolic of the church just as Enoch in the Old Testament was. Jesus will be declaring war on an ungodly earth so He will call his ambassadors home with a trumpet call.

Maybe come up here. **1 Thessalonians 4:13-18 King James Version (KJV)**

13 But I would not have you to be ignorant,
brethren, concerning them which are asleep, that
ye sorrow not, even as others which have no
hope.

14 For if we believe that Jesus died and rose again,
even so them also which sleep in Jesus will God
bring with him.

15 For this we say unto you by the word of the
Lord, that we which are alive and remain unto
the coming of the Lord shall not prevent them
which are asleep.

16 For the Lord himself shall descend from heaven
with a shout, with the voice of the archangel, and
with the trump of God: and the dead in Christ
shall rise first:

17 Then we which are alive and remain shall be
caught up together with them in the clouds, to
meet the Lord in the air: and so, shall we ever be
with the Lord.

[18] Wherefore comfort one another with these words

1 Thessalonians 5

The Day of the Lord

1 Now, brothers and sisters, about times and dates we do not need to write to you,

2 for you know very well that the day of the Lord will come like a thief in the night.

3 While people are saying, "Peace and safety," destruction will come on them suddenly, as labor pains on a pregnant woman, and they will not escape.

4 But you, brothers and sisters, are not in darkness so that this day should surprise you like a thief.

5 You are all children of the light and children of the day. We do not belong to the night or to the darkness.

6 So then, let us not be like others, who are asleep, but let us be awake and sober.

7 For those who sleep, sleep at night, and those who get drunk, get drunk at night.

8 But since we belong to the day, let us be sober, putting on faith and love as a breastplate, and the hope of salvation as a helmet.

9 For God did not appoint us to suffer wrath but to receive salvation through our Lord Jesus Christ.

10 He died for us so that, whether we are awake or asleep, we may live together with him.

11 Therefore encourage one another and build each other up, just as in fact you are doing.

Final Instructions

12 Now we ask you, brothers and sisters, to acknowledge those who work hard among you, who care for you in the Lord and who admonish you.

13 Hold them in the highest regard in love because of their work. Live in peace with each other.

14 And we urge you, brothers, and sisters, warn
those who are idle and disruptive, encourage the
disheartened, help the weak, be patient with
everyone.

15 Make sure that nobody pays back wrong for
wrong, but always strive to do what is good for
each other and for everyone else.

16 Rejoice always,

17 pray continually,

18 give thanks in all circumstances; for this is
God's will for you in Christ Jesus.

19 Do not quench the Spirit.

20 Do not treat prophecies with contempt

21 but test them all; hold on to what is good,

22 reject every kind of evil.

23 May God himself, the God of peace, sanctify
you through and through. May your whole spirit,
soul and body be kept blameless at the coming of
our Lord Jesus Christ.

24 The one who calls you is faithful, and he will do it.

25 Brothers and sisters, pray for us.

26 Greet all God's people with a holy kiss.

27 I charge you before the Lord to have this letter read to all the brothers and sisters.

28 The grace of our Lord Jesus Christ be with you.

We may very well be on the verge of God calling His ambassadors home. If you are reading this book and never accepted Jesus as your savior and
Lord you can do so today. Romans 10: **8** But what
does it say? "The word is near you, in your mouth and in your heart" (that is, the word of faith
which we preach): **9** that if you confess with your mouth the Lord Jesus and believe in your heart that God has raised Him from the dead, you will
be saved. **10** For with the heart one believes unto righteousness, and with the mouth confession is
made unto salvation. **11** For the Scripture says, "Whoever believes on Him will not be put to
shame." **12** For there is no distinction between

Jew and Greek, for the same Lord over all is rich to all who call upon Him. [13] For "whoever calls on the name of the LORD shall be saved."

We know the church does not go through the book of revelation. The only place the church is mentioned is in the first 5 chapters. The church is not mentioned from chapter 6 through to chapter 17. Chapter five shows the 24 elders which is symbolic of the church casting their crowns before Jesus.

FIVE CROWNS AND REWARDS IN HEAVEN.

1.**The Crown of Righteousness:**

(Those who love intimacy with God. Who long for and look forward to the appearing of Jesus. Being with Jesus. Hearts Afire!)

"For I am already being poured out as a drink offering, and the time of my departure has come. I have fought the good fight, I have finished the race, I have kept the faith.
There is reserved for me in the future the crown of righteousness, which the Lord, the righteous

Judge, will give me on that day, and not.

only to me, but to all those who have loved His appearing."
2 Timothy 4:8

2. **The Crown of Life:**

For those who have been faithful through trials, sufferings and even martyred unto death. "Martyr's crown."

"Blessed is the one who endures under trial because, having stood the test, that person will receive the crown of life that the Lord has promised to those who love Him." James 1:12

"Do not fear what you are about to suffer. Behold, the devil is about to throw some of you into prison, that you may be tested, and for ten days you will have tribulation. Be faithful unto death, and I will give you the crown of life."

Revelation 2:10

(death...I will give you Life... opposite)

3. **The Crown Incorruptible (Imperishable)**
(For those who discipline, deny themselves and endure.)
The Victor's Crown.

"Do you not know that those who run in a race all run, but only one receives the prize? Run in such a way that you may win.
Everyone who competes in the games trains with strict discipline. They do it for a crown (garland) that is perishable, but we do it for a crown that is imperishable (incorruptible). So, I do not run aimlessly; I do not box as one beating the air.
But I discipline my body and keep it under control, lest after preaching to others I myself should be disqualified."
I Corinthians 24-27

4. **The Crown of Glory:**
(Those who are servant shepherds of followers of Jesus.)
"Shepherd's crown"

"Shepherd the flock of God that is among you, exercising oversight, not under compulsion, but willingly, as God would have you; not for shameful gain, but eagerly; not domineering over those in your charge, but being examples to the flock.
And when the chief Shepherd appears, you will receive the unfading crown of glory." I Peter 5:2-4

5.**The Crown of Rejoicing**:
(For those who have been a part of evangelism and soul winning.) "Soul winner's crown"

"For what is our hope or joy or crown of rejoicing (boasting) our Lord Jesus at His coming? Is it not you?"
I Thessalonians 2:19

"Therefore, my brethren, whom I love and long for, my joy and crown, stand firm in the Lord, my beloved."
Philippians 4:1

The Foundation:

"For no one can lay a foundation other than that which is laid, which is Jesus Christ.
Now if anyone builds on the foundation with gold, silver, precious stones, wood, hay, straw.
Every man's work shall be made manifest: for the day shall declare it, because it shall be revealed by fire; and the fire shall try every man's work of what sort it is.
If any man's work abide which he hath built thereupon, he shall receive a reward.
If anyone's work is burned up, he will suffer loss, though he himself will be saved, but only as by fire. (Through fire; snatched from the fire; escaping through the flames)" 1 Corinthians 3:11-15

Judgment Seat of Christ

"For we must all appear before the judgment seat of Christ, so that each one may receive what is due for what he has done in the body, whether good or evil." 2 Corinthians 5:10

Treasures in Heaven

"Lay not up for yourselves treasures upon earth, where moth and rust doth corrupt, and where thieves break through and steal: But lay up for yourselves treasures in heaven, where neither moth nor rust doth corrupt, and where thieves do not break through nor steal." Matthew 6: 19-20

They Cast their Crowns before the throne!

"Day and night they never cease to say,
"Holy, holy, holy, is the Lord God Almighty,
who was and is and is to come!"
And whenever the living creatures give glory and honor and thanks to him who is seated on the throne, who lives forever and ever, the twenty-four elders fall down before him who is seated on the throne and worship him who lives forever and ever. They cast their crowns before the throne, saying,
"Worthy are you, our Lord and God,
to receive glory and honor and power,

for you created all things,
and by your will they existed and were created."
Revelation 4:8-11

The elders were singing the song of the redeemed **Revelation 5:9-10** [9]And they sang a new song, saying: "You are worthy to take the scroll and to open its seals, because you were slain, and with your blood you purchased for God persons from every tribe and language and people and nation. [10]You have made them to be a kingdom and priests to serve our God, and they will reign on the earth."

The next time the church is seen is According to **Rev. 17:14** the Church will accompany Jesus to Earth. But in **Rev. 19** He goes to fight the final battle accompanied by the Armies of Heaven. They defeat the enemy forces, throw the anti-Christ and false prophet into the lake of fire, and bind Satan. Then in **Rev. 21**, the New Jerusalem, Home of the Church, appears, having come to Earth with the Lord.

7 THE MANIFESTATION OF THE SONS OF GOD

As much as believers in Christ want finally to want to get on with their destinies and hope the rapture happens immediately, we haven't seen the manifestation of the sons of God yet.

The manifestation of The Sons of God means that "**an act of showing the son of God**. So even all creatures are waiting for the Nature of God to create Son. And all creatures are waiting for his stage. Otherwise, they became bondage, corruption, and suffering. Manifestation means **"an act of showing or displaying."** "For [even the whole] creation (all nature) waits expectantly and longs earnestly for God's sons to be made known [waits for the revealing, the disclosing of their sonship]." Romans 8:19. AMP. Clearly, it is saying that nature is waiting for the sons of God to be revealed. The world is waiting ...

Prayer Points On The Manifestation Of The Sons Of God

The Spirit itself beareth witness with our spirit that we are the children of God. Hebrews 1:6. And again when he bringeth in the first begotten into the world, he saith, And let all the angels of God worship him.

THE SONS OF GOD ARE NOW HIDDEN. 1. How? (1) As to their persons ().It is not exactly known in the winter, when the roots lie in the earth, what will appear in the spring. (2) As to their life (Colossians 3:3).They are hidden not only in point of security, as maintained by an invisible power; but in point of obscurity.

The Manifestation Of The Sons Of God: You Are More Than You Seem

“To whom God would make known what is the riches of the glory of this mystery among the Gentiles; which is Christ in you, the hope of glory:” Colossians 1:27

Manifestation of children of God on earth! We see the need of the Church is to let the Holy Spirit work through them. The supreme task of the Church is the evangelism of the word but many times we see the almost impossible task and forget that the Church is the most powerful force on earth because the Church (the people) are the Temple of the Holy Spirit.

Sanctification is the key to the maturing of the sons of God. All born again Christians are sons and daughters of God. All Christians are overcomers in the sense of being regenerated in spirit. Our spirits are regenerated and made righteous at the new birth. The soul of the believer is being sanctified day by day as we take up the cross daily and follow Christ. The body will be fully sanctified at the resurrection of the dead.

In Revelation chapters two and three, Jesus gives messages to the churches of Asia Minor. In His messages to Ephesus, Smyrna, etc. He starts by giving a message to the church and ends by giving a special promise to those who overcome. The implication is that there are those within the *church who follow on to know the Lord in greater consecration and greater sanctification than the rest of the church. Those who overcome will receive greater spiritual privilege and power. I believe that the 144,000 mentioned in Revelation chapters seven and fourteen are the overcomer company of sons of God who will be manifested in great power just before the second coming of Christ.*

In a nutshell the sonship message is the teaching that there is great power beyond the Pentecostal or Charismatic experience and certain believers in the body of Christ will apprehend this greater power and will enter a higher realm of personal holiness and ministry power to bring great deliverance in the end-times.

8 WILL THERE BE AN ENDTIME AWAKENING

Does the bible predict a great end time awakening or a great apostasy? Will there be a falling away or a catching up? Revival or wrath? Will the church leave the world with a whimper, or will the church leave this world system with a shout?

The Holy Spirit is preparing the church for a mighty wave of His manifestation in the earth. People as far as end time events can't agree no matter the cost. We have a group hollering great falling away. Everyone except them is going to back slide and turn against Jesus.

2 Thessalonians 2

New King James Version

2 Now, brethren, concerning the coming of our Lord Jesus Christ and our gathering together to
Him, we ask you, [2] not to be soon shaken in mind
or troubled, either by spirit or by word or by

letter, as if from us, as though the day of Christ
had come. 3 Let no one deceive you by any
means; for *that Day will not come* unless the
falling away comes first, and the man of sin is
revealed, the son of perdition, 4 who opposes
and exalts himself above all that is called God or
that is worshiped, so that he sits as God in the
temple of God, showing himself that he is God.

5 Do you not remember that when I was still with
you, I told you these things? 6 And now you know
what is restraining, that he may be revealed in his
own time. 7 For the mystery of lawlessness is
already at work; only He who now restrains *will
do so* until He is taken out of the way. 8 And then
the lawless one will be revealed, whom the Lord
will consume with the breath of His mouth and
destroy with the brightness of His coming. 9 The
coming of the *lawless one* is according to the
working of Satan, with all power, signs, and lying
wonders, 10 and with all unrighteous deception
among those who perish, because they did not
receive the love of the truth, that they might be
saved. 11 And for this reason God will send them

strong delusion, that they should believe the
lie, 12 that they all may be condemned who did
not believe the truth but had pleasure in
unrighteousness.

Stand Fast

13 But we are bound to give thanks to God always
for you, brethren beloved by the Lord, because
God from the beginning chose you for
salvation through sanctification by the Spirit and
belief in the truth, 14 to which He called you by
our gospel, for the obtaining of the glory of our
Lord Jesus Christ. 15 Therefore, brethren, stand
fast and hold the traditions which you were
taught, whether by word or our epistle.

16 Now may our Lord Jesus Christ Himself, and our
God and Father, who has loved us and
given *us* everlasting consolation and good hope
by grace, 17 comfort your hearts and establish you
in every good word and work.

We will look at some of the words in 2 Thessalonians chapter two and try to get a clearer picture of the sign less event called the pre-tribulation rapture which is next on God's list of events. When we look at what is going on in the earth it looks like the book of revelation also known as the time of Jacobs trouble or the day of the Lord where God finally settles accounts with Israel and brings judgment on an unbelieving world. With this event looming before us how much more the pre-tribulation rapture is imminent and expected to happen. The area that causes controversy is in verse three **Let no one deceive you by any means; for *that Day will not come* unless the falling away comes first, and the man of sin is revealed, the son of perdition.** The pre wrath, mid-trib, post-trib folks are very narrow in their interpretation of the term falling away.

The "falling away" is the Greek word is *apostasia* and it refers to people's changing their loyalty or allegiance, disobeying established authority.

Because *apostasia* is derived from the verb *aphistēmi* which means "to depart," some Christians assert that this verse is referring to the Rapture. It is also stated that since *apostasia* is preceded by the definite article, “the,” in the Greek, that it must be referring to the well-known departure, the Rapture. But it is a mistake to insist that the meaning of a noun (in this case *apostasia*) is basically the same as the verb (in this case *aphistēmi*) as some commentators have done. As more and more secular Greek documents are unearthed by archaeologists and historians it is clear that it often occurs that nouns, verbs, adjectives, and adverbs, even when from the same root, have very different meanings. This is especially the case when a certain inflection of a word takes on a special meaning, usually referred to by scholars as a “technical meaning,” and that is exactly what has happened with the noun *apostasia*, as Friberg states in his lexicon.

There has been much discussion on what “the apostasy” is that Paul is writing about. This “apostasy” is not about Christians leaving the Christian Faith. From Paul’s teaching and what Daniel says, this “apostasy” is what opens “the Day of the Lord,” the Great Tribulation, and is after the Rapture, so it cannot be about Christians because they will have been Raptured off the earth into heaven. This apostasy is about

the Jews (including deceived Jewish believers) leaving God and His commands and turning to worldly ways to get the support they want. Specifically, it refers to the Jews making a covenant with the man who turns out to be the Antichrist.
The word apostasy is used 15 times in the New Testament but only three times in the context of leaving the faith. It is however used 12 times in the context of leaving a place. The Geneve 1599 bible does not use falling away but departure. The first 5 English translation used the word departure. This debate will be settled not by men but the appearing of Jesus.

Revelation 3:10 — The New King James Version (NKJV) 10 **Because you have kept My command to persevere**, I also will keep you from the hour of trial which shall come upon the whole world, to test those who dwell on the earth.

In order to keep you from the testing that is to come on the whole world we have to be in a different place where we won't be affected by that which is plaguing the whole world. That place is not in the world. **John 14:1-3** NKJV "Let not your heart be troubled; you believe in God, believe also in Me. In My Father's house are many mansions; if it were not so, I would have told you. I go to prepare a place for you. And if I go and prepare a place for you, I will come again and receive you to Myself; that where I am, there you may be also.

Jesus proclaimed the rapture when He told His disciples that He was coming back to receive them to Himself. Where is Jesus? He is in heaven at the right hand of the Father. If Jesus was talking about His second coming, He would have said where you are I shall come to be with you.

From verses 5-9 the lawlessness one or man of sin cannot be revealed until the restrainer is taken out of the way. He (the restrainer) is the body of Christ the believers in Christ in fellowship with the Holy Spirit that is preventing the man of sin to be revealed who Jesus will destroy. And then the lawless one will be revealed, whom the Lord will consume with the breath of His mouth and destroy with the brightness of His coming. People should just stop arguing and realize the appearing of Jesus is different than the coming of Jesus. The appearance is for the Church and the coming is with the church.

1 Thessalonians 5:9-11

New King James Version

[9] For God did not appoint us to wrath, but to obtain salvation through our Lord Jesus
Christ, [10] who died for us, that whether we wake or sleep, we should live together with Him.

[11] Therefore comfort each other and edify one another, just as you also are doing.

Jesus at the cross took the wrath of God for sin and sickness and all forms of bondage that separated us from God the Father. If we had to go through the wrath again thus the time of Jacobs trouble, then we would put Jesus back on the cross because He didn't get it right the first time. To have any other view than pre-tribulation rapture how can you comfort and edify each other if you have torture martyrdom and wrath to look forward to while you are going through a time that doesn't even mention the church after Revelation chapter 4. The church is obviously missing in the earth while the book of Revelation is playing out.

EPILOGUE

Even though in the natural all looks bleak and weary. Practice looking through the eyes of faith. We have a bright and glorious future ahead of us. For the born-again believer what we go through on the earth can be considered hades or torments because we have a glorious future in the presence of Jesus. The unbeliever can only think of this world system as experiencing as much of heaven as they can. They only look forward to an eternity in a lake of fire.

Will you my brothers and sisters in Christ do as much as you can to change the destines of as many unbelievers, within your sphere of influence, as you can?

ABOUT THE AUTHOR

William is a kind considerate person with a heart for people and fears God. His desire is to be an encourager to the body of Christ. To use all the gifts given him to edify exhort and comfort all within the sphere of his influence.

www.ingramcontent.com/pod-product-compliance
Lightning Source LLC
LaVergne TN
LVHW091108150826
845673LV00002B/753

* 9 7 8 1 9 9 0 3 6 2 2 1 7 *